# Australia

## Tradition, Culture, and Daily Life

### MAJOR NATIONS IN A GLOBAL WORLD

# Books in the Series

# Australia

## Tradition, Culture, and Daily Life

### MAJOR NATIONS IN A GLOBAL WORLD

John Perritano

Mason Crest

Mason Crest
450 Parkway Drive, Suite D
Broomall, PA 19008
www.masoncrest.com

Printed and bound in the United States of America.

9 8 7 6 5 4 3

Series ISBN: 978-1-4222-3339-9
ISBN: 978-1-4222-3340-5
ebook ISBN: 978-1-4222-8580-0

The Library of Congress has cataloged the hardcopy format(s) as follows:

Library of Congress Cataloging-in-Publication Data

Perritano, John.
  Australia / by John Perritano.
    pages cm. -- (Major nations in a global world: tradition, culture, and daily life)
  Includes index.

  ISBN 978-1-4222-3340-5 (hardback) -- ISBN 978-1-4222-3339-9 (series) -- ISBN 978-1-4222-8580-0 (ebook)
  1. Australia--Juvenile literature. 2. Australia--Social life and customs--Juvenile literature. I. Title.
DU96.P465 2015
994--dc23
                                    2015005022

Developed and produced by MTM Publishing, Inc.
        Project Director      Valerie Tomaselli
        Copyeditor           Lee Motteler/Geomap Corp.
        Editorial Coordinator   Andrea St. Aubin

Indexing Services          Andrea Baron, Shearwater Indexing

Art direction and design by Sherry Williams, Oxygen Design Group

# Contents

## KEY ICONS TO LOOK FOR:

**Words to Understand:** These words with their easy-to-understand definitions will increase the reader's understanding of the text, while building vocabulary skills.

**Sidebars:** This boxed material within the main text allows readers to build knowledge, gain insights, explore possibilities, and broaden their perspectives by weaving together additional information to provide realistic and holistic perspectives.

**Research Projects:** Readers are pointed toward areas of further inquiry connected to each chapter. Suggestions are provided for projects that encourage deeper research and analysis.

**Text-Dependent Questions:** These questions send the reader back to the text for more careful attention to the evidence presented there.

**Series Glossary of Key Terms:** This back-of-the book glossary contains terminology used throughout this series. Words found here increase the reader's ability to read and comprehend higher-level books and articles in this field.

View of a giant tingle tree at the Valley of the Giants Tree Top walk in the Walpole-Nornalup National Park near the city of Walpole in Western Australia.

# INTRODUCTION

You wouldn't be wrong if you called Australia a continent, an island, or a country. Located in the Southern Hemisphere between the Pacific and Indian oceans, Australia is the world's smallest continent, largest island, and sixth largest country. It stretches about 2,300 miles (3,700 km) from north to south and 2,485 miles (4,000 km) east to west.

Officially known as the Commonwealth of Australia, the country is divided into six states—New South Wales, Victoria, Queensland, South Australia, Western Australia, and Tasmania, an island off the country's southeastern coast. Although Europeans first set eyes on Australia in 1770, the country's earliest inhabitants were there thousands of years before.

Because of its remote location, Australia was isolated for most of its history. That's why a number of plants and animals are only indigenous to the country, including the koala bear and platypus.

Australia is also a study in varying and mesmerizing landscapes that include the Great Barrier Reef, with its 1,200 miles (1,931 km) of living coral, and the vast and rugged Outback, with its magnificent rock formations.

Port Arthur prison in Tasmania.

# WORDS TO UNDERSTAND

**debauchery**: unrestricted, immoral behavior.

**immigrants**: people from one country who move to another region or country.

**magistrate**: a judge who presides over a lower court.

**mores**: established customs.

**petty**: minor, unimportant.

# CHAPTER 1

# History, Religion, and Tradition

Once she realized what the judge had in mind, Elizabeth Beckford might have wished that the executioner had tied a noose around her neck and sent her falling from the gallows. Elizabeth, seventy, stood before the English **magistrate** expecting to be executed for stealing twelve pounds of Gloucester cheese—a hangable offense. The judge, in an apparent show of mercy, ordered Elizabeth to be sent halfway around the world to the desolate British penal colony called New South Wales, in what is today Australia.

In 1770, James Cook, a British naval officer and explorer, landed on the continent, claiming it for England. Eventually, the English were looking for a place to send their convicts and relieve the country's overcrowded prisons.

New South Wales was just the place. It was desolate, barren, a wilderness surrounded by ocean.

And so it was that in 1787 Beckford boarded one of the eleven ships, known to history as the First Fleet, for the seven-month voyage to Australia. Most of the convicts—about 1,000 in all, including males and females—were pale and malnourished and in chains when they left port. Yet, from all accounts, there was a lot of drinking and **debauchery** on the voyage by both convicts and sailors.

## PETTY CRIMINALS

All the prisoners on the 1787 voyage that landed in Australia were petty crooks. There was not a murderer, rapist, political prisoner, or kidnapper among them. Elizabeth Powley, for example, stole a "few shillings" worth of bacon, flour, and raisins and "24 ounces weight of butter." James Grimes, eleven, purloined a bit of ribbon and silk stockings. William Francis stole a book.

*The First Fleet: Entering Port Jackson, January 26, 1788,* lithograph by E. Le Bihan (1888).

An oil painting by Algernon Talmage (1939) depicting Captain Arthur Phillip and the British discovery of present-day Australia.

Commanding the expedition was Captain Arthur Phillip, who had been tapped to become Australia's first governor. Some 252 days after leaving Portsmouth, England, the First Fleet anchored at Botany Bay in New South Wales. Four days after that, Phillips moved everyone to a better location he named Sydney. On January 26, Captain Phillips raised the British flag, and on February 7, 1788, New South Wales was formally proclaimed a British colony.

New South Wales was a hard country for the new colonists. Crops failed, illness struck. The prisoners often fought with each other, sometimes with dire consequences. Life was so bad for Dorothy Handland, the oldest to make the voyage, that she hanged herself from a gum tree. She was eighty-four.

The convicts—160,000 in all would be transported to Australia over several decades—labored to build roads and bridges. By no means were the English alone, however. The continent's first inhabitants, known as Aborigines, had arrived about 30,000 years before from Southeast Asia. Australia's Aboriginal clans spent their days fishing, hunting, and gathering berries and other fruit.

By the 1820s, many more English settlers—including non-convicts—arrived and established settlements in what is now Western Australia. Most were people of means and were able to buy land. They built settlements in New South

*Group of Natives of Tasmania* by Robert Dowling, oil on canvas (1859).

Wales and Van Diemen's Land. But some set out into the interior of the country hoping to find good grazing fields for sheep and other livestock that they brought with them from England. While some of these explorers found excellent pastureland, much of the interior was desolate and harsh.

Nevertheless, wherever settlements thrived, they were free of government control, and the settlers did as they pleased. To control the spread of the settlements, in 1826 Australia's governor decreed the colony would not grant or sell permits to any settler who wanted to move 149 miles (240 km) beyond Sydney. Many people, however, ignored the governor and "squatted" on large tracts well beyond the boundary. These squatters tamed inland Australia.

Cave stencils in the Carnarvon Gorge depict "dream time" stories, which are central to Aboriginal mythology.

## A FERTILE LAND

Most squatters settled on fertile land by rivers and creeks. They established grazing areas for cattle and sheep. Although they did not own the land, they built huts and small out buildings. They fenced off acre after acre to prevent dingoes, a doglike animal, from attacking livestock at night. By the mid-1800s, six of Australia's settlements were thriving.

Things changed tremendously when gold was discovered near Bathurst, New South Wales in 1851. Thousands flocked to the creek from Sydney and elsewhere in the colony, hoping to strike it rich. In August, prospectors discovered an amazingly rich find in Victory, in the Buninyong Range.

World spread quickly well beyond the continent, and by the end of the year, prospectors from as far away as Britain, Scotland, Ireland, Germany, the United States, and China all set sail for Australia. Within a decade, Australia's population doubled. Although the first arrivals were brash men with little regard for the law, more professional traders and skilled craftsmen arrived with middle-class **mores** and families.

As in other colonized regions and countries, settlers and prospectors saw the native people as obstacles. As the Europeans moved farther inland, they displaced the Aboriginal tribes and brought with them diseases that often killed the natives.

## RESERVATION NATION

Ever since Australia was first populated by the British in the late 1700s, white settlers tried to impose their own customs and values on the Aboriginal people. The British forced many of the tribes onto reservations. Although the Native Australians were told they could live on that land forever, they were pushed off these reservations by whites, forcing many Aboriginal people to the cities in search of work and shelter.

Bernard Holtermann with gold "nugget," 1872.

This oil painting by Eugene von Geurard (1853) shows Ballarat's tent city after the discovery of gold in the area.

The governor of Queensland reads the proclamation that established the modern nation of Australia on January 1, 1901, at the Treasury Building in Brisbane, Queensland.

In 1891, the time had come to transform the colony to a nation. During that year, the Australians wrote a constitution. Seven years later, they wrote another one, which was approved by voters and the British Parliament. On January 1, 1901, the new Commonwealth of Australia was born, still part of the United Kingdom, but independent in many ways. Thirteen years later, Australians fought alongside the British and their allies during World War I (1914–1918), and later during World War II (1939–1945).

World War II was a precarious time as the Japanese threatened the continent. By the spring of 1942, the Japanese had conquered the Philippines, Burma, Malaya, and the Dutch East Indies with little resistance. By the end of April, the Japanese wanted to seize control of the Coral Sea, located between Australia and New Caledonia. They planned on invading Port Moresby in southeastern New Guinea, which would leave Australia isolated and open to attack.

Luckily, the Americans had broken the Japanese secret code and learned of the plan. On the morning of May 7, American and Japanese carrier groups faced each other in the Battle of the Coral Sea. When it was over the next day, the Americans had stopped the invasion of Port Moresby and halted any Japanese attempt to invade Australia.

After the war, Australia became increasingly active in world affairs. It was an original member of the United Nations, and it sent troops to Korea during the Korean War. It also opened up its door to European **immigrants** displaced by World War II.

At the time, the government paid many immigrants to settle in Australia. In return, the newcomers had to work at whatever jobs the Australians gave them for two years. Not only did immigrants come from Germany, but many also escaped Soviet-dominated Eastern Europe. Today many of the new arrivals come from Asia, including China, Cambodia, and Vietnam. Some 6.5 million people have immigrated to Australia since 1945.

# TEXT-DEPENDENT QUESTIONS

1. What was the name given to the eleven ship convoy that carried the first British convicts to Australia?

2. When did Australia officially become a commonwealth?

3. What is a squatter?

# RESEARCH PROJECTS

1. With a group of classmates, use the Internet and the library to research stories about the first British convicts who came to Australia. Select one, then write a Reader's Theater play about the trials they faced colonizing a new land. The play could include parts for a narrator, three convicts, a colonial governor, and two members of an Aboriginal tribe.

2. Research and compare the treatment of Native Americans by the United States government and the treatment of Aboriginal Australians by the Australian government. List some of the comparisons and differences. What can you conclude?

St. Mary's Cathedral in Sydney, New South Wales.

Australia's annual kite-flying festival.

# WORDS TO UNDERSTAND

**counteract**: to prevent something from having an effect.

**hierarchal**: relating to a ranking system, with defined places for those at the top, middle, and bottom.

**kinship**: web of social relationships that have a common origin derived from ancestors and family.

**lyricism**: emotional and enthusiastic expression of feelings.

# CHAPTER 2

# Family and Friends

"G'day mate!"
Translation: "Hello, my friend."

Australians are many things, but more than anything else, they come across as a relaxed and informal people. Most dress in casual clothes, such as open-necked shirts, shorts, and jeans. Perhaps it's because of the warm climate, or perhaps it's because Australians seem to take life a bit more slowly than the rest us.

The Australian penchant for being nonchalant is reflected in their speech, which is peppered with a variety of slang terms that gives their brand of English a whimsical **lyricism**. For example:

Aussie is a person from Australia.

Barbie means barbecue.

Bludger is a person who works very little or not at all.

Bonza is a word for excellent.

Dinky-di is a person who seems genuine.

Jackarro defines a male who works with horses.

## MANY LANGUAGES

Australia is a nation of immigrants, a blend of established cultures, Aboriginal people, and new influences. More than 200 different languages and dialects are spoken in the country, including forty-five indigenous languages.

Australians, for the most part, enjoy one of the highest standards of livings in the world. Seventy-five percent of the country's 23 million or so people live along the coast. Most people own their own homes and many drive an automobile.

Like most families in modern, developed societies, Australian children grow up in two-parent families, although in recent years more people have been opting to live alone without marrying. Indigenous households are larger and are more likely to be headed by one parent.

Celebrating Christmas Eve at the St. Mary's Cathedral in Sydney.

Degraves Street, one of Melbourne's well-traveled pedestrian walkways, attracts friends and family to its bars and restaurants.

The Australian family has undergone major shifts recently. Like many countries, including Germany and Japan, Australia's population is aging and people are not having children as often as they did. Moreover, many people live alone. In fact, the average household size in Australia has declined from 3.6 people per household in 1954 to 2.5 today.

### FAVORITE PUBS

Many Australians socialize with their friends in crowded pubs. If someone offers to "shout it," they are not going to yell at you. Instead, he or she is offering to buy a person a drink. Laws prohibiting drinking and driving are tough and rigorously enforced by police.

Despite these demographics, family and friends are central to the average Australian. One of the most cherished activities that bonds family and friends occurs in the dead of summer during Christmas. It's called Carols by Candlelight when families and friends come together under the stars and sing Christmas carols. Many of the homes they visit are decorated with palm leaves, evergreens, and colorful flowers including the Christmas bush and Christmas bellflower.

In fact, Christmas is probably one of the most important times of the year, when families re-create the traditions of their ancestors, many of whom came to Australian from somewhere else. Australians of Irish descent observe many of the traditions of Ireland, such as placing a candle in the front window to welcome Mary, Joseph, and the baby Jesus. The youngest child then lights the candle. Going to midnight mass is also an important part of the season.

Christmas Day is a time for families and friends to grill their Christmas dinner on the barbie. Some families will even go to the beach, where Father Christmas often shows up in shorts. In fact, with most Australians living near the coast, one of the unique aspects of life is the country's beach culture. Australia has a thriving beach culture, where people meet, play, and relax.

The origins of the beach culture date back to the late 1800s, when hotels and guesthouses dotted the coast. Piers soon followed and by the 1920s, a seaside lifestyle began to emerge, taking off in the 1950s as people had access to automobiles, which made the beaches an easy commute. The guesthouses of the 1880s gradually became a relic of the past, as people began building camping grounds. Many families today still stay in these beachside resorts during the summer. As the cities grew, so did the beaches. They became a sanctuary for the laid-back and casual Aussie.

Sydney's Bondi Beach, an example of Australia's laid-back beach culture.

This stamp from 1950 depicts Gwoya Jungarai, an Aboriginal elder of the Walibri people.

About 500 Aboriginal groups call Australia home. The Aborigines have complex social relationships. Families are based on the **kinship** system, which determines how family members react and behave toward one another. Kinship defines who will look after a child if a parent dies and who can marry whom. Kinship also dictates who is responsible for another person's debts or misdeeds and who will care for the sick.

## ABORIGINAL MARRIAGE CUSTOMS

In many Aboriginal societies, a man cannot marry a woman unless he undergoes a long initiation process, one that can take years. Most of the time, a man's first wife is the widow of an older man, although subsequent wives can be much older. In some tribes, a marriage can occur if a woman simply walks through a camp or village to meet a man at his request.

Aboriginal culture also places a huge emphasis on tribal elders. Aboriginal communities have a **hierarchal** structure, with elders ranked on top. They are selected for their compassion, courage, and knowledge of tribal law. They also lead the group during times of conflict and advise the young on selecting marriage partners. Village elders are mostly male and often take care of the tribe's sacred objects. Women also have a special role in society in the tribe and gain power and status as they age. Like men, women carry out separate religious rituals.

Medicine men are important components of Aboriginal society. Medicine men are healers. Not only do they diagnose and cure illnesses (usually by ritual magic). They hold séances to connect to deceased ancestors and conduct investigations when someone dies unexpectedly or by unexplained circumstances.

A man drawing "dream time" symbols, based on Aboriginal mythology, in the sand.

Some Aboriginal groups might also have sorcerers, who practice so-called black magic. They cast spells on people of other tribes, unfaithful wives, and others. Many people are afraid of the sorcerer and will often call a medicine man to **counteract** a black magic spell.

Storytelling is one of the most important aspects of Aborigines' lives. It is a source of literature and history. Riddles, narratives, proverbs, and other oral tales pass down useful knowledge about the tribe, their land, and their culture. Many of the stories are shared publically, but others are only told in private. Some stories are only meant for men; others for women. Stories are used in certain ceremonies, gatherings, or as part of initiation rites.

## FUNERAL RITES

In Aboriginal tribes, funerals and other mourning rituals are extreme affairs. Those who have lost a loved one might slice their foreheads or burn themselves with hot coals. Sometimes a family might move from the area, while in other families the bereaved might not speak to anyone for a long time.

# TEXT-DEPENDENT QUESTIONS

1. Describe the role of elders in Australia's Aboriginal society.

2. Why do you think Australia's "beach culture" was able to flourish?

3. What's a jackarro?

# RESEARCH PROJECTS

1. Use the Internet to research these Australian slang terms: cashed up, cobber, fair dinkum, and arvo. Next, use them in a sentence. Then, compare them to similar terms you might use when talking to friends.

2. Research and read several Aboriginal stories. As you read, keep in mind that these stories were meant to be spoken. Study how each is crafted. Many have morals or a greater truth. Finally, create a story of your own. Write it down and read it to the class.

A little girl making friends with a kangaroo during a family outing at a park.

Grilled rib-eye steak, from Wagyu cows, a popular breed of cattle in Australia.

# WORDS TO UNDERSTAND

**currency**: a system of money.

**eclectic**: varied.

**gastronomic**: relating to quality cooking or dining.

**generic**: general; not specialized.

# CHAPTER 3

# Food and Drink

Australia, home of immigrants and a thriving indigenous population, has one of the world's more **eclectic** contemporary cuisines. From Vegemite sandwiches to good 'ole fish and chips, Australia's **gastronomic** scene reflects a multicultural society that draws together flavors and styles from many traditions.

Dating back to precolonial times, Aboriginal Australians lived off the land, hunting emus, kangaroos, moths, lizards, and snakes. They also picked berries, dug roots, and searched for honey. They fished, catching numerous types of seafood.

When British settlers arrived, they found a bounty of food that they did not recognize. Some were familiar, such as fish, geese, and pigeons. Others were not as well known, nor were they popular. To make Australia seem more like home, the British planted familiar crops and brought animals from the homeland. They hunted deer. They fished and planted orchards and vineyards, where they pressed grapes into wine.

An Australian meat pie with ketchup.

In those early days, Australia lacked a proper cuisine. "No other country on earth offers more of everything needed to make a good meal, or offers it more cheaply than Australia," wrote journalist Edmond Marin La Meslee in 1883. "But there is no other country either where the cuisine is more elementary, not to say abominable."

Things slowly changed. Over the next two hundred or so years, a blended style of Australian cookery began to emerge. Yes, the British-style of cooking was still popular: cooks created dishes such as shepherd's pie, roast beef with Yorkshire pudding, Cornish pastries, apple pie, and fish and chips. Now, however, immigrants from other parts of the world began to leave their mark.

During the gold rush days of the mid-1800s, many of those who traveled to Australia were Chinese. They brought with them their own style of cooking, which varied throughout China. The Chinese came to prospect for gold but soon realized that mining was a tough way to make a living. Instead, they started growing vegetable gardens that supplied settlers with food. These market gardens flourished in northwest Australia.

## WORLD WAR BISCUITS

Biscuits are immensely popular. For instance, Anzac biscuits, named in honor of the Australian and New Zealand Army Corps (ANZAC), which fought in World War I, were first made by wives during the war and sent to the soldiers fighting in Europe. The women made the biscuits from rolled oats, flour, sugar, coconut, syrup, butter, water, and bicarbonate of soda, which preserved the treats on their long sea voyage.

Anzac biscuits.

After World War II, Australia opened its doors to immigrants from Europe, including those from Greece and Italy. They brought with them their own culinary traditions. In the 1970s, immigrants from Japan, Vietnam, Cambodia, and other Asia nations moved to the continent as well, influencing the way people ate. In recent years, Australian food has developed a decidedly Middle Eastern flavor.

While immigrant chefs continue to create delectable dishes, Australia's cuisine is also heavily influenced by region and climate. Australia has many environments, which cooks use to add flare to many dishes, especially seafood. Surrounded by water, Australia has an abundant supply of fish, crustaceans, and other types of edible creatures. The seas vary from warm to a bit chilly, adding to the variety.

In Queensland, diners are served mud crabs, reef fish—such as the highly regarded red emperor snapper—coral trout, and pearl perch. In the Northern Territory, barramundi, commonly called Asian sea bass, is very popular. The residents of Sydney dine on oysters and yellowfin tuna, while on the island of Tasmania, where the sea is cool, deep-sea crabs, scallops, and rock lobster are favorites.

Roasted barramundi fish is popular in the Northern Territory.

An Australian barbeque with sausages and rissoles, or patties.

### LET THEM EAT LAMINGTON

Everyone loves cake, and in Australia they adore lamington, which the Aussies refer to as the "National Cake of Australia." Lamington is a square-shaped sponge cake with chocolate icing and bits of coconut.

However, nothing says "dinner" in Australia more than barbeque. At the center of a barbie, or barbeque, are Australian snags, or sausages made of traditional pork or beef and flavored with various herbs.

Australians eat all types of meat, and gourmet cooks are eager to serve kangaroo, crocodile, and buffalo. Kangaroo, once a delicacy, is now a prime entrée. The filets are low in fat and high in protein. Before cooking, chefs often marinate the meat in oil for at least fifteen minutes, because kangaroo dries out when it is cooked. Kangaroo can be tossed into a variety of dishes including a pastry pie with mushrooms, kangaroo burgers, and kangaroo chili.

Traditional Australian sponge cake called lamington.

Emu is also on the menu. These long-necked birds are mostly fat free and low in cholesterol. Their meat is high in iron and can be served smoked, cold, or as a pizza topping. Some chefs have taken the emu and made a pie out of its meat, complete with feta cheese, sun-dried tomato, onion, and black pepper.

The classic Australian spread Vegemite on a slice of fresh bread.

## VEGEMITE SANDWICHES

Vegemite is a dark-brown food paste made from leftover brewers' yeast. Although most people don't really know the ingredients, the paste is seasoned with spices, various vegetables, and other additives. In the 1980s, the musical group Men at Work introduced the world to the Vegemite sandwich, when they mentioned it in one of their songs, "Down Under." At the time the song was recorded, the sandwich had been around nearly sixty years.

Australia abounds in dairy farms, especially in Tasmania, King Island, and Kangaroo Island. In these and other areas, cheese is king. In the 1970s, expert cheese makers began producing cheese of fine quality that they then exported around the world.

While some cheeses go by the **generic** names of cheddar and brie, many are named for their place of origin, including Mersey Valley and Milawa Blue cheese. There is even a cheese flavored with gum leaves. Today, Australia exports 500,000 tons of dairy products annually, and cheese contributes $1 billion in Australian **currency** to the economy.

Modern Australian dishes also depend on ingredients that have been part of the country for thousands of years. The Aborigines have a special bond with the land, and their knowledge of food has been passed from one generation to another. Australia's first settlers dismissed the Aborigines as simple people, but what they didn't know is that many indigenous tribes irrigated land to grow crops and managed and maintained a vast stock of food resources.

A shop at the Victoria Market in Melbourne selling cheeses and meats.

Many Aboriginal dishes are eaten raw, but others are cooked, pounded, and roasted. Among the most popular are those made from witchetty grubs, which are fat, white, squirming caterpillar-like creatures mostly found in the central part of the country. The grubs live below ground, feeding on the roots of trees, and are hard to find. People eat the grubs raw, or chefs can cook them with cheese, creamed-style corn, and almonds.

Witchetty grubs are part of some traditional Aboriginal dishes.

# TEXT-DEPENDENT QUESTIONS

1. How did the Chinese come to manage market gardens in Australia?

2. Explain how different cultures influenced Australia's cuisine.

3. Identify and describe three different indigenous foods.

# RESEARCH PROJECTS

1. Choose seven meals that you have eaten over the past week. Which of these dishes would you associate with the cuisines of other countries? Create a list of the ingredients used in each of those dishes. Next, identify those ingredients with other countries. Write a two-page summary that describes the impact other cuisines have on your eating patterns.

2. Imagine that a friend will be traveling to Australia. He or she wants information on what types of food to expect. Go online and research different recipes from Australia. Create a meal planner for your friend, which includes three or four dishes they can eat at breakfast, lunch, and dinner. Make sure you include different types of beverages, and perhaps a section on snacks.

Freshly cooked Australian prawns.

The Royal Arcade in Melbourne.

# WORDS TO UNDERSTAND

**exploitation**: the use or development of something, especially natural resources, to gain a benefit.

**disperse**: distribute over a large area.

**fiscal**: relating to monetary matters.

**private sector**: part of a free market economy made up of companies and organizations that are not owned or controlled by the government.

# CHAPTER 4

# School, Work, and Industry

Australia completed its twenty-first consecutive year of economic growth at the end of 2013. No other economy—not that of the United States, Japan, or China—can boast such a thing. Despite the ups and downs of the world's economy over the past two decades, Australia has been able to weather **fiscal** crisis after fiscal crisis, including the most recent worldwide recession that strangled many economies beginning in 2007.

Australia has been able to survive and prosper because of its vast natural resource reserves, a thriving agricultural economy, a robust manufacturing industry, and a highly educated and skilled workforce. In 2012, Australia was ranked eighth out of forty-eight countries in the quality of its higher-education system, behind only the United States, Canada, Sweden, Finland, Denmark, Switzerland, and Norway.

## VACATIONING DOWN UNDER

In recent years another sector of the Australian economy has taken off—tourism. In 2013, tourists spent nearly $80 billion, up 11.4 percent since 2009. The Outback, the Great Barrier Reef, and Sydney are popular tourist destinations. People can also visit the Daintree Rainforest, located in northern Queensland. It's the largest rainforest in the country and home to 30 percent of Australia's reptile and marsupial species. It also contains 20 percent of the country's bird species.

The ranking system, complied by researchers at the University of Melbourne's Institute of Applied Economic and Social Research, ranked each nation based on such things as government and **private sector** investment in higher education and the amount and type of research each university conducted.

Divers explore the Great Barrier Reef, a main attraction of Australia's tourism industry.

With a literacy rate of 99 percent, Australia's education system is strong. Students, like those in many other countries, must stay in school for twelve years before graduating to a university. Every classroom, from primary school to high school, includes students of the same age. Those who have trouble learning are put into special classes to give them the help they need.

Most students start their schooling at the age of five. Those who are younger often attend "Child Care" centers or participate in "Family Day Care," a government-approved form of child care in which children go to the homes of educators. The educators work closely with regulators who monitor the progress of the students.

Top-notch high school education in Australia includes a solid foundation in the sciences.

The last two years of high school are considered extremely important for those wishing to attend a university or college. During those years, students are evaluated and ranked as they tailor their classes toward their chosen professions. For example, those who want to study engineering at a university will take classes in physics and high-level mathematics, instead of history or biology.

In addition to public school, Australia has a number of schools run by various religious denominations, most notably the Roman Catholic Church. Still, as in other nations, the government has responsibility over these and other private schools. In Australia, state and territorial governments have the responsibility to oversee and fund education. Each is also responsible for the education of Aboriginal students.

In the past, Aboriginal students were treated as second-class citizens. In the early 1800s, Aboriginal children were taught to be laborers and servants to white colonial families. Some students were forcibly separated from their parents and brought to these schools.

During the second half of the nineteenth century and the early twentieth century, the government created Aboriginal reserves—land set aside for indigenous tribes. The Aborigines were forced to live on these reservations while

Aboriginal students on their way to school in Alice Springs, in the Northern Territory.

their children were pulled from their parents, as they were earlier, and placed in special schools so they could be trained as domestic servants and laborers.

Some Aboriginal students had the opportunity to attend public school with non-Aboriginal children, but school administrators could refuse admittance if white parents objected. As a result, the government was forced to build schools just for Aboriginal students. Most were substandard.

It wasn't until the 1950s and 1960s that the government closed the unequal Aboriginal schools and opened the state-run schools to indigenous students. Today, inequities still exist. When compared to non-Aboriginal students, Aboriginal students often experience a variety of problems. Aboriginal tribes are dispersed in a large and often remote geographical area, which makes educating students difficult. Many Aboriginal children do not speak English. These factors and others have made educating Aboriginal children extremely difficult.

Australia's economy does not rely on one industry but is highly diversified. Although there is little fertile land on the continent, Australia is a major producer and exporter of many agricultural products. Most of the 134,000 farms are family-owned, and each farmer produces enough food to feed 600. Moreover, Australian farmers produce 93 percent of the country's food supply and export around 60 percent of what they grow and produce.

## FOLLOWING THE SHEEP

The Aussies have historically been a nation of sheepherders, producing more than half of the world's wool. Sheep are found in all regions in the following numbers: Western Australia (15.5 million); South Australia (10.8 million); New South Wales (27.9 million); Queensland (2.9 million); Tasmania (2.4 million); and Victoria (16.1 million).

Wheat is one of the largest cash crops in the country. Farmers sow wheat in autumn and reap it spring or summer depending on weather conditions. The states of Western Australian, New South Wales, South Australian, Victoria, and Queensland are the country's largest wheat producers. Most Australian wheat is exported overseas to Asia and the Middle East. Japan, Vietnam, South Korea, Malaysia, and Indonesia are the largest buyers of the crop.

Wine is also an important industry. When the first Europeans arrived, there were no native grapes grown in Australia and consequently no grapes to make wine. One of the first things the colonists did was to import grapes from Europe and then export wine to England.

Today, Australia is dotted with sixty wine-producing regions. Because the country has varied climates, winemakers can produce both red and white wines in sweet, dry (nonsweet), and sparkling varieties. In fact, there is so much wine-making going on that the country now is a major exporter of the intoxicating beverage. In fact, Great Britain imports most of its wine from Australia, rather than just across the English Channel from France.

Mining is another major industry. The discovery of large gold deposits in the 1850s opened the door to the **exploitation** of various minerals. Australia is the world's leading producer of bauxite (the principal ore of aluminum), nickel, uranium, zinc, lead, and other minerals. It is also second in world in the

A flock of sheep grazes near Albany in Western Australia.

Harvesting grapes on a vineyard in the Southern Highlands.

The Super Pit is one of the largest open-pit gold mines in the country.

mining and production of copper, gold, iron ore, and silver and the third largest producer of diamonds.

## THE SUPER PIT

The gold mine in Kalgoorlie, in the state of Western Australia, is one of the largest in the country. Known as the Super Pit, it runs continuously, seven days a week, with a big blast at one in the afternoon resulting in a massive harvest of gold daily.

Like other developed nations, Australia's manufacturing runs the gamut from automobile factories to plastic manufacturers to drug makers. In 2013, Australia exported $3.8 billion worth of automobiles and parts, mostly to the Middle East and North America. Domestically during that same year, Australians spent $1.13 billion on cars and trucks, a 2.2 percent increase from 2012. The country's chemical and plastic industries represent 10 percent of the country's industrial output, employing more than 50,000 people.

# TEXT-DEPENDENT QUESTIONS

1. How many farms are there in Australia?

2. What are some of Australia's main natural resources?

3. What is Australia's literacy rate?

# RESEARCH PROJECTS

1. Use the Internet or library to research one of the two schools that Aboriginal children were forced to attend (Cootamundra Domestic Training Home for Aboriginal Girls and Kinchela Aboriginal Boys Training Home) and then write a short essay about what life was like in the school for these children.

2. Research agriculture in Australia and create a table of data about three important crops in the country. Include items such as locations of major production, yearly production volume, and percent of total agricultural production.

A sheep shearer in Queensland gathers wool.

A surfer in the Southport
Gold Coast, Queensland.

# WORDS TO UNDERSTAND

**behemoth**: gigantic; large.

**commission**: the awarding of a job or project to an artist, designer, or other professional.

**condemned**: issued an official order saying a building is unfit to be used.

**subjugation**: the act of forcing a people or nation to do something they do not want to do.

# CHAPTER ⑤

# Arts and Entertainment

In 1979, when ESPN launched, it wasn't the **behemoth** sports network that it is today. Although the founders of the network dreamed one day of broadcasting professional football, basketball, and baseball games, there was no chance of that happening immediately. At the time, the network televised little-known sports, including Australian Rules Football. Americans tuned in by the thousands. More than thirty years later, ESPN still broadcasts the sport.

The Aussies are crazy about their football, which is nothing like American-style football, or even soccer for that matter. Australian football is a cross between rugby, soccer, and American football and perhaps a bit of basketball (players can bounce the ball if they wish). In fact, many think that Austra-

The Western Bulldogs play Australian-rules football against the Richmond team.

lian football encapsulates the perceived ruggedness of Australian society. For one thing, the game illustrates the toughness and bravado of male Aussies. The players don't wear pads or helmets, and they move the ball by running and punching it forward. They can kick it too, if they so choose. Players frequently smash into one another, often with abandon. With no protective gear, blood is sometimes drawn. Not only are there big hits, but sometimes a brawl can break out.

A team scores when a player kicks the ball through massive field goalposts. Unlike American football, there are two sets of poles. Kick it through the middle and players score six points. Miss, but make it through the smaller outer set, and the team tallies one point.

Australians also love their athletes. The tennis player Rod Laver is remembered by many. He won twice all four Grand Slam Titles (Australian Open, French Open, Wimbledon, and U.S. Open) in one year, once as an amateur the other as a pro. Swimmer Betty Cuthbert won three gold medals in the 100 meter, 200 meter and 4X100 relay in the 1956 Melbourne Summer Olympics.

## AT THE MOVIES

Many Australian movies have entertained theatergoers across the globe for years. Two of the most iconic include *Mad Max*, starring Mel Gibson, and *Crocodile Dundee*, which was such a hit that tourism in Australia increased after the film's release.

Another popular competitive sport, with its own World Cup, is boomerang tossing, which has its roots in the country's Aboriginal history. During a boomerang tournament, throwers compete in many different events. They stand in the center of several concentric circles and let the boomerang fly. The ultimate test of a thrower's prowess is the Aussie Round, in which the boomerang is expected to cross the 164 foot (50 m) circle and come right back.

A painted boomerang.

Gaelic football and hurling also have deep historical roots: they can be traced, at least in Australia, to the 1840s when a newspaper reported a Gaelic football game played in South Australia. The game's actual origins go back to ancient Ireland. It is played between two teams of fifteen players on a grass pitch, or field. The players try to score by hurling the ball through the other team's goals. Unlike Aussie football, the Gaelic football is round like a soccer ball, but slightly smaller. Players can kick, bounce, or pass the ball to advance it up the field.

From its time as a colony, Australia has had a mix of ethnicities, each with its own customs, celebrations, and leisure-time activities. The country's huge Chinese population made the celebration of Chinese New Year an important event in Australia. Street festivals, food, dancing, and music are all hallmarks of the New Year.

The Greeks, many of whom came to Australia after World War II, added their own influence by celebrating St. Basil's Day, an Orthodox Christian holiday, at the start of the new year. In many Greek homes, a cake is baked on the eve of the feast day, with a gold or silver coin hidden inside. According to tradition, the person who gets the piece of cake with the gold piece will have good luck for the whole year.

A father and son dance with a group of Aboriginal performers at a wildlife sanctuary.

In January, Australia's German community participates in Schützenfest, an annual celebration held in Adelaide, the capital of South Australia. In the 1830s, German immigrants, most of whom were Lutheran, migrated to Australia. To keep their culture alive, they held Schützenfest, a competitive shooting competition popular in the homeland. The first Schützenfest in Australia was held in 1865. Today the festival is marked not only by competitive target shooting but also with dancing, food, and drink.

Perhaps the biggest celebration is Australia Day, January 26. The day commemorates the arrival of Captain Arthur Phillips and the eleven ships of convicts he commanded in 1788. Although it celebrates the arrival of British colonists, many in the indigenous community look at Australia Day as the beginning of their **subjugation** at the hands of the Europeans. While the past is still remembered, most Australia Day celebrations today are multicultural events.

### DANCING WITH THE ABORIGINES

Music means a lot to the Aborigines. It is how people learn their culture and how they fit into their natural world. Children are taught to dance when they are very young. When they reach puberty, children learn the first songs about plants and animals that are important to the tribe or clan. The songs are not written but are passed down orally.

In another throwback to British influence, Australians celebrate Boxing Day on December 26. The day was originally held so the wealthiest people in the British Commonwealth could help the less fortunate by providing them gifts of money, food, and clothing. The gifts were usually packed in boxes, which is where the day

A busy Bondi Beach on Boxing Day, December 26.

gets its name. In Australia, people spend the day at the beach, while many businesses hold massive after-Christmas sales.

Many Australians love to go to the theater and to musical concerts. One of the most iconic buildings in Australia is the Sydney Opera House, with its distinctive roof of interlocking vaulted "shells." The first Sydney Opera House opened in 1879 and was later **condemned** in 1900. Forty-seven years later, an English composer, Eugene Goossens, said that Sydney needed a new opera house for the Sydney Symphony Orchestra.

Celebrating Australia Day in Sydney.

## THE DIDGERIDOO AND CLAPSTICKS, TOO

Each tribe has a variety of musical instruments, many of which are made from wood. One of the most famous is the didgeridoo, a wind instrument. Many Aboriginal tribes also use boomerang clapsticks, which are curved wooden blades. A person grips the clapsticks in the center, one in each hand, and raps them together.

The Opera House—framed beautifully by the azure water of Sydney Harbor—opened in 1973. Designed by Jørn Utzon, a relatively unknown architect at the time of his **commission**, the Opera House is so unique that is on the UNESCO's (United Nations Educational, Scientific and Cultural Organization's World Heritage) preservation list, which notes that it "represents multiple strands of creativity, both in architectural form and structural design, a great urban sculpture . . . and a world famous icon building."

A member of the Australian band OKA plays the didgeridoo.

The Sydney Opera House in Sydney Harbor.

# TEXT-DEPENDENT QUESTIONS

1. Which immigrant community celebrates the Schützenfest?

2. Explain the concept behind Boxing Day.

3. Describe a tradition associated with the celebration of the Greek Orthodox holiday of St. Basil's Day.

# RESEARCH PROJECTS

1. One of Australia's most famous movies is a Mel Gibson film titled *Gallipoli*. The film was named for a famous battle in World War I. Research that battle and write a short report including information about the commanders, the site, the battle's objectives, and the importance of the battle in the outcome of the war.

2. Research and compare the rules of Australian football with American-style football. Create a chart that shows the similarities.

Similar to this festival in Hanover, Germany, the German community of Adelaide, South Australia, celebrates Schützenfest.

Story Bridge over the Brisbane River in Brisbane, Queensland.

# WORDS TO UNDERSTAND

**cosmopolitan**: worldly; showing the influence of many cultures.

**emblazoned**: decorated with.

**endemic**: native, or not introduced, to a particular region and not naturally found in other areas.

**hub**: center of activity.

**inhospitable**:  harsh; unwelcoming.

# CHAPTER 6

# Cities, Towns, and the Countryside

Australia is vast—roughly the size of the continental United States—with low mountains, level plains, and broad plateaus. It has rich fertile land and red rock desert, big cities full of culture and arts, and vast rural stretches with little or no population.

The continent has a wide range of climates. The northern third of the country is tropical, while the south is more temperate. Summers, which take place during the Northern Hemisphere's wintertime, are hot and rainless, but in the winter and spring, the wind blows from the west, drenching parts of Western and Southern Australia, as well as Victoria, New South Wales, and Tasmania, making those regions good for farming.

Melbourne is famous for its pedestrian walkways and shopping arcades.

Sydney, the site of the first British settlement, is Australia's best-known city, and with more than 4.5 million people, its most populous. Located in New South Wales, Sydney is a **cosmopolitan** city, one whose skyline is jaw-dropping. With its sandy beaches, it is the center of Australian colonial history and culture and the **hub** of fashion and cuisine. The city has a huge immigrant population.

Surrounded by sprawling suburbs, Sydney is compact, an amalgamation of six neighborhoods including City Centre, home to many attractions, shopping, restaurants, and offices; The Rocks, which includes the colonial village of Sydney and its Harbour Bridge; City South, where Chinatown is located; and City East, the center of the city's nightlife.

The city of Melbourne is not just the financial and government center of Australia, but it has been ranked many times as the world's most livable city. One reason for that designation is that Melbourne is the center of the nation's art and culture scene.

Moreover, two unique aspects of Melbourne are its pedestrian walkways and shopping arcades, including the Block Arcade, which has a mosaic-tiled floor. It was built between 1891 and 1893 and is now packed with cafes and boutiques. Centre Place, or Degraves Street, is another popular shopping and dining area decorated by street art and graffiti.

Yet, when people conjure images of Australia, their mind often goes quickly to the Outback. The Outback, or "bush," is the sprawling and remote interior of Australia. It covers millions of square kilometers of desert, including portions of the Northern Territory, South Australia, West Australia, and Queensland. It is a vast and expansive region, with rocky hills, flood plains, and caves **emblazoned** with Aboriginal art.

When the first colonists arrived, they settled along the coast. By the 1860s, however, people began moving inland, traversing the continent from one end to the other. The Outback makes up about 70 percent of Australia's landmass, but only about 3 percent of the country's population lives there.

In the Outback, paved roads are few, so traveling by car or truck is very difficult. In fact, many families fly from one town to the next. Because the Outback is very dry, wildfires and droughts are common. Yet, the Outback is a treasure trove of minerals, with huge iron ore deposits, gold, and silver.

## LIVING IN THE OUTBACK

The Outback is the center of Aboriginal life. Most traditional Aboriginal housing was simple, often made from branches covered with leaves or sheets of bark, depending on what was available from the environment. Today, many Aboriginals live in modern brick homes.

Ancient art in the Yourambulla Caves depicts emu and kangaroo.

A traditional Aboriginal hut.

Although rugged and **inhospitable**, the Outback is an awe-inspiring landscape. Chief among the natural landforms is Ayers Rock—a sandstone formation 1,142 feet (348 m) high with a circumference of 5.8 miles (9.4 km). In 1873, surveyor William Gosse became the first white person to see Australia's most recognizable landform.

Called Uluru by the Aborigines, the rock rises from the northern Australia desert floor, looking down over the hot and dry lowlands. The Aborigines consider Uluru a sacred outcropping, and there are many examples of historic Aboriginal art from those that occupied the region centuries ago.

The Outback is not the only place in Australia with mesmerizing scenery. Located off the eastern coast is the Great Barrier Reef, the largest formation of coral in the world. Coral is formed by millions of tiny sea animals, whose limestone exoskeletons build the reefs and remain when they die. The Great Barrier Reef, which stretches some 1,800 miles (2,900 km), runs almost parallel to the coast and encompasses 134,363 square miles (348,000 sq km).

---

## WONDERLAND OF WILDLIFE

The Great Barrier Reef is teeming with wildlife. Scientists have recorded thirty-six species of whales, dolphins, and porpoises, while six species of sea turtles come to the reef to breed. There are about 215 bird species that nest or roost on the islands. Moreover, about 10 percent of the world's total fish species can be found within the reef. Although vast, the Great Barrier Reef is in danger from climate change, coral bleaching, and pollution.

---

An aerial view of Ayers Rock, or Uluru.

Colorful fish and coral in the rich habitat of the Great Barrier Reef.

The Great Barrier Reef is home to the world's largest collection of coral and is a playground for various fish, including more than 1,500 different types of tropical fish. It is also home to many mollusk species and sponges, along with dolphins and other marine mammals. The reef also includes more than 900 islands and a variety of birds, reptiles, and other animals.

## WHAT IS CORAL?

Thousands of tiny coral polyps make up coral. As the polyps take in calcium from seawater and chemically link it with carbon and oxygen, a white skeleton of calcium carbonate forms. Each polyp attaches itself to another polyp with a flat piece of soft tissue.

Australia teems with wildlife, the likes of which cannot be found anywhere else on the planet. Geographically isolated by thousands of miles of ocean, many species are **endemic** to the island continent. Among them is the platypus, a mammal that lays eggs.

Most of the world's marsupials—that is, pouched animals—are located in Australia, including the kangaroo, wombat, and koala. Interestingly, marsupials first evolved in North America and found their way to Australia by crossing into South America and Antarctica.

A young koala in a eucalyptus tree.

Today, 140 species of marsupials are found nowhere else but in Australia. The smallest, the long-tailed planigal, weighs less than an ounce; the largest, the red kangaroo, can weigh 209 pounds (95 kg). One of the most distinctive marsupials is the tree-dwelling koala, which dines only on the leaves of eucalyptus trees.

By contrast, the dingo, or wild dog, did come from somewhere else: it was introduced to Australia by Asian sailors some 4,000 years ago, although scientists say the dogs might have arrived perhaps 18,000 years ago. Dingoes can live in many habitats, dining on wallabies, wombats, rabbits, and kangaroos.

### RABBIT RUN

Rabbits, goats, water buffalo, foxes, and even camels were introduced to Australia by Europeans. Rabbits, which were first brought over in the 1850s, multiplied quickly, overrunning the country.

Perhaps no one animal is as synonymous with Australia as the kangaroo. The Aborigines hunted the kangaroo for the animal's meat and skins. When the first settlers arrived, they too hunted kangaroo in order to survive. The animal is not a threatened species and the most populous of the pack include the red, eastern grey, and western grey kangaroos.

A kangaroo explores a backyard in the countryside.

# TEXT-DEPENDENT QUESTIONS

1. Name three different marsupials indigenous to Australia.
2. Explain how Australia's isolation allowed various species of animals to thrive only on that continent.
3. Explain how coral reefs form.

# RESEARCH PROJECTS

1. Research the dangers facing the Great Barrier Reef and create a computer slideshow, complete with text and photographs that explain many of the dangers.
2. Pick one of the animals from the text. Create a poster with pictures and text showing where in Australia that animal lives, what it eats, whether it has any predators, and whether it is threatened.

The "Three Sisters" in the Blue Mountains of New South Wales.

# FURTHER RESEARCH

## Online

The Australian Geographic Society's website (http://www.australiangeographic.com.au/) has info on food, news, and the outdoors, with vivid photography at each turn.

The "About Australia" page on the Australia's government website (http://www.australia.gov.au) is a gateway to info about the country's culture, government, and people, among other material.

The Central Intelligence Agency's World Fact Book on Australia provides up-to-date statistics, a short history, and maps: https://www.cia.gov/library/publications/the-world-factbook/geos/as.html.

The "About the Great Barrier Reef" page (http://www.greatbarrierreef.org/about.php) of the web magazine GreatBarrierReef.org (http://www.greatbarrierreef.org) offers insight and images on all aspects of this natural wonder.

Aboriginal culture can be explored at Survival's website (http://www.survivalinternational.org/tribes/aboriginals).

Find out more about Australian culture at http://www.dfat.gov.au/facts/people_culture.html.

## Books

Flood, Josephine. *The Original Australians: Story of the Aboriginal People.* Sydney: Allen & Unwin, 2007.

Smith, Roff. *Australia.* 5th ed. Des Moines: National Geographic, 2014.

Welsh, Frank. *Australia: A New History of the Great Southern Land.* New York: Overlook Press, 2008.

NOTE TO EDUCATORS: This book contains both imperial and metric measurements as well as references to global practices and trends in an effort to encourage the student to gain a worldly perspective. We, as publishers, feel it's our role to give young adults the tools they need to thrive in a global society.

# SERIES GLOSSARY

**ancestral**: relating to ancestors, or relatives who have lived in the past.

**archaeologist**: a scientist that investigates past societies by digging in the earth to examine their remains.

**artisanal**: describing something produced on a small scale, usually handmade by skilled craftspeople.

**colony**: a settlement in another country or place that is controlled by a "home" country.

**commonwealth**: an association of sovereign nations unified by common cultural, political, and economic interests and traits.

**communism**: a social and economic philosophy characterized by a classless society and the absence of private property.

**continent**: any of the seven large land masses that constitute most of the dry land on the surface of the earth.

**cosmopolitan**: worldly; showing the influence of many cultures.

**culinary**: relating to the kitchen, cookery, and style of eating.

**cultivated**: planted and harvested for food, as opposed to the growth of plants in the wild.

**currency**: a system of money.

**demographics**: the study of population trends.

**denomination**: a religious grouping within a faith that has its own organization.

**dynasty**: a ruling family that extends across generations, usually in an autocratic form of government, such as a monarchy.

**ecosystems**: environments where interdependent organisms live.

**endemic**: native, or not introduced, to a particular region, and not naturally found in other areas.

**exile**: absence from one's country or home, usually enforced by a government for political or religious reasons.

**feudal**: a system of economic, political, or social organization in which poor landholders are subservient to wealthy landlords; used mostly in relation to the Middle Ages.

**globalization**: the processes relating to increasing international exchange that have resulted in faster, easier connections across the world.

**gross national product**: the measure of all the products and services a country produces in a year.

**heritage**: tradition and history.

**homogenization**: the process of blending elements together, sometimes resulting in a less interesting mixture.

**iconic**: relating to something that has become an emblem or symbol.

**idiom**: the language particular to a community or class; usually refers to regular, "everyday" speech.

**immigrants**: people who move to and settle in a new country.

**indigenous**: originating in and naturally from a particular region or country.

**industrialization**: the process by which a country changes from a farming society to one that is based on industry and manufacturing.

# SERIES GLOSSARY

**integration**: the process of opening up a place, community, or organization to all types of people.

**kinship**: web of social relationships that have a common origin derived from ancestors and family.

**literacy rate**: the percentage of people who can read and write.

**matriarchal**: of or relating to female leadership within a particular group or system.

**migrant**: a person who moves from one place to another, usually for reasons of employment or economic improvement.

**militarized**: warlike or military in character and thought.

**missionary**: one who goes on a journey to spread a religion.

**monopoly**: a situation where one company or state controls the market for an industry or product.

**natural resources**: naturally occurring materials, such as oil, coal, and gold, that can be used by people.

**nomadic**: describing a way of life in which people move, usually seasonally, from place to place in search of food, water, and pastureland.

**nomadic**: relating to people who have no fixed residence and move from place to place.

**parliament**: a body of government responsible for enacting laws.

**patriarchal**: of or relating to male leadership within a particular group or system.

**patrilineal**: relating to the relationship based on the father or the descendants through the male line.

**polygamy**: the practice of having more than one spouse.

**provincial**: belonging to a province or region outside of the main cities of a country.

**racism**: prejudice or animosity against people belonging to other races.

**ritualize**: to mark or perform with specific behaviors or observances.

**sector**: part or aspect of something, especially of a country's or region's economy.

**secular**: relating to worldly concerns; not religious.

**societal**: relating to the order, structure, or functioning of society or community.

**socioeconomic**: relating to social and economic factors, such as education and income, often used when discussing how classes, or levels of society, are formed.

**statecraft**: the ideas about and methods of running a government.

**traditional**: relating to something that is based on old historical ways of doing things.

**urban sprawl**: the uncontrolled expansion of urban areas away from the center of the city into remote, outlying areas.

**urbanization**: the increasing movement of people from rural areas to cities, usually in search of economic improvement, and the conditions resulting this migration.

# INDEX

*Italicized page numbers* refer to illustrations.

# INDEX

# INDEX

# INDEX

# PHOTO CREDITS

| Page | Page Location | Archive/Photographer | Page | Page Location | Archive/Photographer |
|---|---|---|---|---|---|
| 6 | Full page | Dreamstime/Rene Drouyer | 30 | Top | Dreamstime/Tktktk |
| 8 | Top | Dreamstime/Instinia Photography | 30 | Bottom right | Wikimedia Commons/Sputnikcccp |
| 10 | Bottom | Wikimedia Commons/E. Le Bihan | 31 | Bottom | Dreamstime/Matthew Trapp |
| 11 | Top | Wikimedia Commons/Algernon Talmage | 32 | Top | Dreamstime/Tktktk |
| 12 | Top | National Gallery of Australia/Robert Dowling | 34 | Bottom | Dreamstime/Sburel |
| 12 | Middle right | Wikimedia Commons | 35 | Top right | Dreamstime/Photographerlondon |
| 13 | Bottom left | Wikimedia Commons/State Library of New South Wales | 36 | Top | iStock.com/fotofritz16 |
| | | | 37 | Bottom left | Dreamstime/David Steele |
| 13 | Bottom right | Wikimedia Commons/Eugene von Guerard | 37 | Bottom right | Dreamstime/Phillip Minnis |
| | | | 38 | Top | Dreamstime/Gillespaire |
| 14 | Top left | Wikimedia Commons/John Oxley Library | 39 | Bottom | Dreamstime/Lucidwaters |
| | | | 40 | Top | Dreamstime/Katerinasamsonova |
| 15 | Bottom | Dreamstime/Barissonmez | 42 | Top | Dreamstime/Max Blain |
| 16 | Top | Dreamstime/Vselenka | 43 | Top right | Dreamstime/Pannawish Jarusilawong |
| 18 | Bottom | Dreamstime/Kapilsabharwal | 44 | Top | iStock.com/kokkai |
| 19 | Top | Dreamstime/Lucidwaters | 45 | Top right | Dreamstime/Daniel Krzowski |
| 20 | Bottom | Dreamstime/Duncan Sharrocks | 45 | Bottom | iStock.com/brians101 |
| 21 | Top right | iStock.com/Linde1 | 46 | Top right | Dreamstime/Piyus Silaban |
| 22 | Top | iStock.com/kerriekerr | 46 | Bottom | Dreamstime/Markus Gann |
| 23 | Bottom | Dreamstime/Nataliya Tiedemann | 47 | Bottom | Dreamstime/Julia Bauer |
| 24 | Top | Dreamstime/Paul Cowan | 48 | Top | Dreamstime/Lucidwaters |
| 26 | Top right | Dreamstime/Robyn Mackenzie | 50 | Top | Wikimedia Commons/Rae Allen |
| 26 | Bottom right | Dreamstime/Robyn Mackenzie | 51 | Bottom left | Dreamstime/Mark Higgins |
| 27 | Bottom | Dreamstime/Twilightartpictures | 51 | Bottom right | Dreamstime/Ben Mcleish |
| 28 | Top | iStock.com/MarkPiovesan | 52 | Bottom | Dreamstime/Joshua Cortopassi |
| 28 | Middle right | Dreamstime/Robyn Mackenzie | 53 | Top | Dreamstime/Pniesen |
| 29 | Top right | Dreamstime/Jabiru | 54 | Top left | Dreamstime/Michael Elliott |
| | | | 54 | Bottom | Dreamstime/Martingraf |
| | | | 55 | Bottom | Dreamstime/Hotshotsworldwide |

## COVER

| | |
|---|---|
| Top | Gerald Reisner |
| Bottom left | Dollar Photo Club/Kristian Ahrent |
| Bottom right | Dollar Photo Club/Ashwin |

# ABOUT THE AUTHOR

**John Perritano** is an award-winning journalist, writer, and editor from Southbury, Connecticut, who has written numerous articles and books on history, culture, and science for publishers that include National Geographic's *Reading Expedition Series* and its *Global Issues Series*, focusing on such topics as globalization, population, and natural resources. He has also been a contributor to Discovery.com, *Popular Mechanics*, and other magazines and websites. He holds a master's degree in American History from Western Connecticut State University.